THINKING BIBLICALLY ABOUT

THE iPOD...

BRIAN DRAPER

CONNECT: THINKING BIBLICALLY ABOUT THE iPOD...

Copyright © Brian Draper 2007
First published 2007
ISBN 978 1 84427 280 8

Scripture Union, 207–209 Queensway, Bletchley, MK2 2EB, England.
Email: info@scriptureunion.org.uk
Website: www.scriptureunion.org.uk

Scripture Union Australia
Locked Bag 2, Central Coast Business Centre, NSW 2252
Website: www.scriptureunion.org.au

Scripture Union USA
PO Box 987, Valley Forge, PA19482
Website: www.scriptureunion.org

British Library Cataloguing-in-Publication Data: a catalogue record of this book is available from the British Library.

Printed and bound in Great Britain by Henry Ling Ltd, Dorchester, England.

Cover and internal design by ie Design of Birmingham, UK

Typesetting by Creative Pages www.creativepages.co.uk

Scripture Union is an international Christian charity working with churches in more than 130 countries providing resources to bring the good news about Jesus Christ to children, young people and families and to encourage them to develop spiritually through the Bible and prayer.

As well as our network of volunteers, staff and associates who run holidays, church-based events and school Christian groups, we produce a wide range of publications and support those who use our resources through training programmes.

CONNECT

John Stott, a former president of Scripture Union, has stressed the need for Christians to 'relate the ancient Word to the modern world.' His vision is for integrated Christians – those who have brought every area of their lives under the lordship of Christ – to penetrate the world. To this end we hope that each booklet in the Connect series will 'do what it says on the tin' – help readers think *biblically* about the big issues of the day. And, having begun to think biblically about those issues, we pray that readers will feel able to thoughtfully penetrate the world, making a biblical perspective part of their everyday conversations about those issues and part of their own everyday living.

Nigel Hopper
Matt Campbell
Series Editors

USING CONNECT

Connect booklets are designed for use by both individuals and small groups. We suggest you first read through the booklet, either as a whole or a chapter at a time, before going back to think again about the questions highlighted in the page margins. You should find that these will give you or your group plenty to think or talk about further. Naturally, we hope that wrestling with these questions will stimulate further, deeper questions of your own and enhance your biblical thinking.

WWW.CONNECTBIBLESTUDIES.COM

Connect booklets are available as PDF downloads from the Connect website. Check the website regularly for details of new and forthcoming Connect titles, as well as other features.

OTHER TITLES IN THE CONNECT SERIES

Connect: Beauty (ISBN 978 1 84427 271 6)
Connect: Climate Change (ISBN 978 1 84427 279 2)

CONTENTS

INTRODUCTION

'iPod, therefore I am.' It could be the mantra for our times. If you commute to work then you'll know that almost everyone has an MP3 player – if not Apple's slick designer model, then one of the many colourful clones and copies – part of the maddening, chirruping chorus breaking up what would otherwise be a collective vow of railway carriage silence.

Today, we glide through our journey of life to our personally selected soundtrack. We rattle through the darkness of the underground to the Arctic Monkeys. We stalk majestic hills to the overtures of Dvořák. We drift into the depths of sleep with Simon and Garfunkel. We psych ourselves up before business meetings with the Red Hot Chilli Peppers. Where would we be without our pocket jukeboxes that provide an endless supply of the right music for the right moment, and contain the musical selection and expression of our own personal taste?

Is it possible that as we increasingly plug into our iPods and so hermetically seal ourselves into a bubble of sound, we're actually changing the way we listen to God's great gift of music?

But is it possible that as we increasingly plug into our iPods and so hermetically seal ourselves into a bubble of sound, we're actually changing the way we listen to God's great gift of music? And is this something that we, as Christians, should be concerned about? This booklet is designed to help you reflect on these and other, related issues, by exploring what it might mean to think *biblically* about music and its role in our lives, and what, therefore, the implications might be for the way we use our iPods or other MP3 players.

1 WHAT'S ON YOUR iPOD AND WHY?

PASSIVE AND ACTIVE LISTENING

Can you remember the first record (yes, record, as in vinyl disc) you ever bought? I can: it was by Showaddywaddy, which is probably as uncool to admit then as it is now. But then we all have musical skeletons in the closet (or the loft, which is where Showaddywaddy ended up), don't we?

However, I can't remember the *last* record (as in, vinyl disc) I bought. It was possibly U2's album, *Zooropa*, in 1992. I know that I graduated to a CD player soon after. It was such a novelty to get a crisper, clearer sound – and not to have to turn the record over. At that point, music ceased to be a game of two halves, two carefully crafted sides, five or six songs in length. It also became so much more convenient, somehow. We stopped listening so deliberately, so proactively. When you stuck a record on, it was an event. Put on a CD and, for some reason, it seems more of a backdrop. And with the advent of the iPod, the sequence of songs is broken up further, into a pick-and-mix selection that we can take wherever we want. True, we may sometimes choose to listen deliberately and carefully to the songs we've chosen for our journey, but aren't we prone all too often to use music as a shapeless comfort-blanket of sound to keep us company, fill the silence and keep the demons at bay?

Aren't we prone all too often to use music as a shapeless comfort-blanket of sound to keep us company, fill the silence and keep the demons at bay?

And music, by the way, really does help to keep the demons at bay. In the Old Testament (1 Samuel 16:14–23), we read of a king who was deeply tormented, and who turned to music to help soothe his troubled spirit. Seeing his torment, King Saul's attendants sought his permission to find a musician whose playing could bring relief during his troubled episodes. Messengers were sent and soon David and his lyre were in Saul's service. And it worked: 'Whenever the spirit from God came on Saul, David would take up his lyre and play. Then relief would come to Saul; he would feel better, and the evil spirit would leave him' (1 Samuel 16:23). Are we to infer, then, that music can have a spiritual presence which lifts our souls towards God and causes our hearts to sing? And can we say that this is true regardless of whether the music that has this impact on us is secular or sacred? And is to regard music as 'just entertainment' to vastly underestimate its power, or even its God-given purpose?

Is to regard music as 'just entertainment' to vastly underestimate its power, or even its God-given purpose?

When we put our iPods on, what are we listening for?

If music has a function, then it's important to ask ourselves, before we proceed any further, how do we use it? When we put our iPods on, what are we listening for? Are we tuning into something – or tuning out the world? Are we turning to music for inspiration – or using it as a brief release from desperation? Is it connecting us to someone, or something greater, beyond ourselves? How does it change our moods, our minds, and our hearts?

2 THE SOUNDTRACK OF OUR LIVES

MUSIC AS SELF-EXPRESSION

A recent survey by Co-operative Funeralcare revealed that the most popular pop song to be played at funerals is Frank Sinatra's recording of 'My Way'. No doubt one reason why many people choose this particular song is that it acts as a kind of celebratory testimony and creates a sense of heroic individualism, of the deceased person's being a 'character'. And this is true whether they chose their own music, or had it chosen for them by their family. Before we start with a standard Christian lament about how it would be so much better if people would pay more attention to living God's way than 'my way', it's worth considering that at least some of the sentiment of the song finds echoes in the Bible.

Psalm 139 reminds us that we are 'fearfully and wonderfully made' (v 14). Expanding on the same idea, in Matthew 10:30 Jesus seeks to inspire courage and confidence among his disciples for their mission by reassuring them of God's care, telling them, '…even the very hairs of your head are all numbered.' Can we not say, then, that the Bible supports the idea of our individuality, teaching that God has created each of us uniquely, with the inevitability that we will live our lives in our own, unique way? Why not make time to listen to 'My Way' in the light of this teaching?

Then, there's the parable of the talents – you'll find it in Matthew 25:14–30 and also in Luke 19:12–27. The master's rewarding of the two servants who risked

Can we not say, then, that the Bible supports the idea of our individuality, teaching that God has created each of us uniquely, with the inevitability that we will live our lives in our own, unique way?

what he gave them to gain more may suggest that what God (the Master) wants is for us to live life with a sense of risk, a swagger, almost, a *joie de vivre*. Perhaps he wants us to live with more of the spirit 'My Way' and less of the fearfulness of the servant who simply buried what he'd been given until the master returned? That said, the emphasis in the parable on the master and his relationship with his servants should probably guard us against developing any understanding of living 'My Way' that is incompatible with serving God's kingdom.

So, in light of this, what song would you like to be played at your funeral? Pause for a moment now to think about it. Ask yourself, why *that* song? What is it about the words, the tune, the sound, and the feel of that song that makes it resonate with your understanding of who you are? Would other people be surprised at your choice? What songs might they expect to hear at your funeral?

In the hit TV show of the 1990s, *Ally McBeal*, each of the main characters had a theme song. Ally's was 'Tell Him':

> *'I know something about love*
> *You've gotta want it bad*
> *If that guy's got into your blood*
> *Go out and get him...'*

John 'The Biscuit' Cage, meanwhile, always turned to Barry White's 'You're My First, My last, My Everything' when he needed to find his inner song:

> *'We got it together, didn't we?*
> *Nobody but you and me.*
> *We got it together, baby.'*

The Bible may not talk about 'theme songs' as such, but it makes it clear that songs play a crucial part in helping us to express who we are – as God's people – through culture. 'How can we sing the songs of the Lord while in a foreign land?' asks the writer of Psalm 137 (v 4). 'Sing to the Lord a new song,' exhorts Psalm 96:1. The songs we sing are clearly important. They

The songs we sing are likely to be those we listen to. Should we therefore think more deeply about what's on our iPod?

orientate us, and reveal something deep about who we are. The songs we sing are likely to be those we listen to. Should we therefore think more deeply about what's on our iPod?

My own theme song, at least for the moment, is U2's 'Walk On'. When I saw them play it live at Earl's Court, it was the final song of a blistering set that brought faith and life together in one continuous stream of music. As I stood there, up the front, Bono sang:

> *'You're packing a suitcase for a place none of us has been*
> *A place that has to be believed to be seen...'*

And my heart glimpsed with the eyes of faith that we are all on a journey toward God. The music lifted me to a place I really hadn't been before, a sacred space which offered me a moment of clarity about how music can be used to pierce the sky and shake our reality and speak to us in ways that words alone can't. And on this occasion it wasn't even what most people would call 'worship music'!

Ever since Elvis Presley started gyrating his hips, Christians have debated whether it's helpful or not to listen music that isn't strictly about God or offering worship to him. But though they may not be a 'worship band' in the conventional sense, don't U2 write from their hearts about faith and life? And don't many other artists also do this, even if they are not Christians?

Isn't it also true that there are plenty of so-called 'Christian' bands who lack the depth or musical gravitas of others?

Isn't it also true that there are plenty of so-called 'Christian' bands who lack the depth or musical gravitas of others? So wouldn't it be unwise to take the view that we should listen only to music that is specifically labelled 'Christian' even if that means excluding the music of artists with something to say or with a sound that might help us to re-imagine our place in the grand scheme of things?

We each have to make our own decision as to what kind of music can elevate us, stretch and challenge us, build us up or move us on. But shouldn't we make that decision on the understanding that 'the Lord's song' doesn't always come through the expected channels, and that the Lord can sing to us in different ways? The next time you sit on the tube, or go for a run, or walk down the street with your headphones on, ask yourself how the music you are listening to has the capacity to help you see the world in a different way. And ask God to speak to you from within different sounds and melodies; from unexpected sources, from within snippets of lyrics or entire overtures. You may just begin dancing in step with the rhythm of life more fully. You may begin singing your own version of 'the Lord's song' within a strange land.

3 JUKEBOX JURY

YOU AND YOUR PLAYLIST

So, what's on your iPod? It's one of those questions that frequently get asked in the magazine sections of our Sunday newspapers. Life is a playlist, and you're in control of the soundtrack.

Today, we can pick and mix our music from an almost infinite array of choice. Walk into a major high-street record shop and it's bewildering enough. Visit the iTunes online store and you may just get overwhelmed by the number of songs you could potentially download, each for just 79p a pop!

And so it is with life. We face so many choices daily, that sometimes it's hard to ever commit to anything whatsoever. If you want a cup of coffee, you're forced to choose between 27 different varieties before you can pay. And if you want religion, there's an awful lot of it on offer out there.

Think, for a moment, about the wide-ranging implications for just about every area of life that are contained in Jesus' assertion that the teaching of the entire Old Testament hangs on the commandments, 'Love the Lord your God with all your heart and with all your soul and with all your mind', and 'Love your neighbour as yourself' (Matthew 22:37–40).

In Matthew 7:14 Jesus says, '…small is the gate and narrow the road that leads to life, and only a few find it.' Can we infer from this that, as Christians, our decision-making should be more disciplined than that of the world around us – that we have a narrower range of options than would normally be on offer? Certainly, the Bible gives us a few simple rules of thumb to live by and on which to base our decision-making. Think, for a moment, about the wide-ranging implications for just about every area of life that are contained in Jesus' assertion that the teaching of the entire Old Testament hangs on the commandments, 'Love the Lord your God with all your heart and with all your soul and with all your mind', and 'Love your neighbour as yourself' (Matthew 22:37–40). Or what about his command, '… love your enemies, do good to those who hate you, bless those who curse you, pray for those who ill-treat you' (Luke 6:27–28)? Or what of the prophet Micah's message to God's people that what is required of them is to '…act justly and to love mercy and to walk humbly with your God' (Micah 6:8)?

Is it the case, then, that when we commit to following Jesus (who is the Way) along his 'narrow way', we find guidance, direction and purpose for our life's journey? A culture with so much choice and room for self-expression, so much potential division and fragmentation, in which we can feel pulled in so many different directions at once, is obviously going to make it difficult for Christians to live with complete integrity. But by providing us with reference-points, with a potential source of purpose and clarity, doesn't commitment to Jesus make it a little easier to assemble the soundtrack of our lives?

By providing us with reference-points, with a potential source of purpose and clarity, doesn't commitment to Jesus make it a little easier to assemble the soundtrack of our lives?

I find that some songs speak intimately to me of the Christian commitment I have made and of the journey of faith that I have embarked upon. U2's 'Walk On', as I mentioned previously, is one; a song overtly concerned with the walk of faith.

Another (which I keep on my iPod at all times) is Moby's short violin piece, 'Now I let it go', which I play every now and again as an accompaniment to a spiritual exercise I do. In my mind, I imagine something I need to relinquish – it might be a bad habit, or something that has hurt me, or that I am holding too tightly to – and then, as I play the piece, I imagine I'm holding it tightly in my fist. As the song proceeds (it has no lyrics) I gradually unfurl my fist and open my hand, and imagine letting the unhelpful thing go. The song really helps me to focus on that moment in time, and on travelling more lightly. So the iPod, for me, potentially helps me to carry such moments around with me wherever I go.

Another song I love is 'Wake Up' by The Arcade Fire, a Canadian band who are on the rise. 'If the children don't grow up,' they sing, 'our bodies get bigger but their hearts get torn up'. It's a song of awakening, a rallying call, a call to grow up and into something bigger. But it's not just the words that get me – the music itself moves me, somehow. It exhilarates me. And that helps to connect my soul to God in a way that I couldn't do otherwise.

'Chasing Cars', by Snow Patrol, is another song that inspires me in a similar way:

> *'Forget what we're told,*
> *before we get too old,*
> *show me a garden that's bursting into life …*
> *All that I am, all that I ever was,*
> *is here in your perfect eyes,*
> *they're all I can see …*
> *I need your grace*
> *to remind me*
> *to find my own.'*

The wealth of choice in our culture flings us a challenge. How should we respond to it, as we make our playlists, select our songs and seek to express ourselves, our beliefs and our tastes in this pick-and-mix world?

But of course, I fill my iPod, as you probably do, with an eclectic mix of sounds I've picked up along the way: dance, trance, folk, rock, indie, classical, 50s, 60s, 70s, 80s, 90s, Noughties... The wealth of choice in our culture flings us a challenge. How should we respond to it, as we make our playlists, select our songs and seek to express ourselves, our beliefs and our tastes in this pick-and-mix world?

4 TURN OFF, TUNE IN

THE SPIRITUAL ART OF SILENCE IN AN iPOD AGE

'Your ears are full but you're empty' – Blur, 'Coffee and TV', from the album, 13

How are your ears? If you're used to playing your MP3 player at full blast, then they're probably ringing. I sat on the bus the other day and the guy next to me was listening to hip-hop so loudly that the whole bus could hear it. As well as being incredibly irritating to everyone else, how can it have been good for him? He didn't have a look of studied concentration or inspiration; instead, he looked zoned out.

The Bible tells us to 'Listen to [God's] voice, and hold fast to him,' (Deuteronomy 30:20). 'Let the wise listen and add to their learning … the fear of the LORD is the beginning of knowledge', commands the writer of Proverbs, in its opening chapter. And then there's the story of Elijah, recorded in 1 Kings 19:1–18. He had fled the threats of the evil queen, Jezebel, and on the way to Horeb had sat down under a tree and wished himself dead. But God provided food and water to sustain him on his journey, and when Elijah finally reached Horeb, he went into a cave and spent the night there…

'The Lord said, "Go out and stand on the mountain in the presence of the Lord, for the Lord is about to pass by."

Then a great and powerful wind tore the mountains apart and shattered the rocks before the Lord, but the Lord was not in the wind. After the wind there was an earthquake, but the Lord was not in the earthquake. After the earthquake came a fire, but the Lord was not in the fire. And after the fire came a gentle whisper. When Elijah heard it, he pulled his cloak over his face and went out and stood at the mouth of the cave' (1 Kings 19:11–13).

What is this remarkable passage about if not the need to listen carefully for the voice of God? But isn't the iPod an icon of our drowned-out, bass-heavy culture, that can so easily make us zone out when we tune in, like that guy on the bus?

What is this remarkable passage about if not the need to listen carefully for the voice of God? But isn't the iPod an icon of our drowned-out, bass-heavy culture, that can so easily make us zone out when we tune in, like that guy on the bus? Therefore, while it's right, as we have seen, to believe that God speaks through music and song, and dances with us to the rhythm of life, aren't there times when we need to switch off from the matrix, times when we need to be still and know that God is God?

Switching off from the white noise of our culture isn't easy; it requires discipline. But, isn't that what discipleship, as the word suggests, is all about? Isn't it through the exercise of discipline that Christians can provide a positive alternative to the prevailing culture? Think about it like this: to resist the temptation to put the TV on automatically is to fight the tide of commercialism and cheap 'drama' that flows into our homes and so into our heads and so into our hearts. To resist the temptation to buy a 'Blackberry' and be on call for your work 24 hours a day is to acknowledge that there's more to life than work. And so can't going for a run without our headphones, for a change, be a means of opening ourselves to the possibility of listening for the still small voice of God? How often do we automatically stick on our iPods and so, automatically, prevent ourselves from listening more actively for the voice of God?

How often do we automatically stick on our iPods and so, automatically, prevent ourselves from listening more actively for the voice of God?

It's worth remembering that even Jesus, who enjoyed perfect communion with God, thought it necessary, on occasions, to withdraw by himself to a quiet place to pray (Luke 5:16) – an activity that's as much about listening to God as it is about talking to him. How much more, then, do we need to do the same? It doesn't have to be very early in the morning, nor need it involve leaving the house (Mark 1:35). If you're feeling over-connected, try this simple ritual: sit by yourself in a room at home and light a candle and lay your iPod at its base, as a symbol that you're resolving for that time to press the 'mute button' of life and soak yourself in silent prayer and reflection.

Why do we need surround-sound and -vision in our lives? One reason, I'd suggest, is boredom. Another is emptiness.

When we're bored, it's easy to descend into lethargy and reach for immediate, passive entertainment rather than creating our own. In one respect, therefore, if we tune out the world by playing music all the time (or by watching TV, or playing computer games), aren't we simply becoming more unimaginative, more uncreative and more uninspired? And doesn't that mean that we're effectively shrinking our soulfulness?

If we tune out the world by playing music all the time (or by watching TV, or playing computer games), aren't we simply becoming more unimaginative, more uncreative and more uninspired? And doesn't that mean that we're effectively shrinking our soulfulness?

However, a deeper malaise in our culture is emptiness. We don't like a lull because we can't face the void. Nothingness equals loneliness equals emptiness. We feel uncomfortable in our own presence – or at least, we have not learned how to be at peace with ourselves – and at the same time, we have not cultivated the art of 'being' within God's presence. There is a huge difference between solitude and loneliness; there is a chasm between stillness and boredom. Is it not the case that the iPod (or whatever our preferred choice of MP3 player may be), if used carelessly, can be a symbol of our fear of the void and our refusal to confront the deeper questions of life – those which whisper to us, perhaps, as we go to sleep at night? Is that why people fall asleep to music as well?

Is it not the case that the iPod (or whatever our preferred choice of MP3 player may be), if used carelessly, can be a symbol of our fear of the void and our refusal to confront the deeper questions of life – those which whisper to us, perhaps, as we go to sleep at night?

David, it seems, had cultivated the art of 'being' within God's presence. Consider, reflectively, peacefully and meditatively, the words of what is perhaps the most well-known of all the Psalms he wrote:

'The Lord is my shepherd, I lack nothing.
He makes me lie down in green pastures,
He leads me beside quiet waters,
He refreshes my soul.
He guides me along the right paths
For his name's sake.
Even though I walk

Through the darkest valley,
I will fear no evil,
For you are with me;
Your rod and your staff
They comfort me.
You prepare a table before me
In the presence of my enemies.
You anoint my head with oil;
My cup overflows.
Surely your goodness and love will follow me
All the days of my life,
And I will dwell in the house of the Lord forever.'

(Psalm 23)

What is this Psalm if not the testimony of a man at peace with himself and in communion with God, the testimony of a man happy to trust that God is leading him into the places that he wants to take him?

5 OK, COMPUTER?

GETTING INTIMATE WITH TECHNOLOGY

Humans and machines, of course, are becoming ever more entwined. Our technology is evolving to become a part of our very being; and today, we are truly wired for sound. The iPod is an icon for our changing notion of humanity. We don't just use technology as a tool in today's culture; instead, technology is fast becoming a central part of who we really are.

We now exist in a technological loop – moving from one item of technology to the next, always connected. We turn off the TV and go to order our groceries on the Internet; as we get into the car, we put our mobile earpiece in and punch our destination's coordinates into the GPS system. We are never far from being online, from being plugged into 'the matrix', if you like. Never far from having broadband-width access to everyone we know, to any music we want to listen to, to any information we need to glean or any person we need to contact.

Who am I within this technological loop? Am I simply me? Or am I stretched, extended and somehow changed by the technology I hook up to?

Who am I within this technological loop? Am I simply *me*? Or am I stretched, extended and somehow changed by the technology I hook up to? At an extreme level, I can take on a completely different alter-ego in games such as *Second Life* or *World of Warcraft*. In many milder forms, we can wrap ourselves in layers of ideas, text, imagery, sound or light; we can shrink space and time, extend our reach and make our presence felt in so many different places at once. When we plug in our iPod, or reach for the phone, don't we, in a way, become wired-in to a hard drive, a portable memory? Don't we have to become part of the circuitry, in order to so dramatically increase our capacity for communication and consumption?

The iPod reminds us just how flexible our lives have become, and how we have so much at our fingertips. On the one hand, this provides a wonderful and welcome freedom, to listen to what we want, when we want – creating the illusion that the music is more than simply portable – it is actually becoming *part of us*. We seem to feel it in our veins, have the songs written onto our brains as if they, too, were a memory stick. On the other hand, doesn't this heady sense of total immersion carry the risk of our being totally enfolded in entertainment – unconsciously sucked into a new way of life, a new world of subliminal messages, of brands and bands and celebrities? You may feel that everything begins to blur and bleed into a 4-D version of MTV. Does life itself become an advert for the iPod world, in which we play our part by wearing the headphones and dancing the dance?

The Bible teaches that, as Christians, we are in the process of being transformed into the image of Christ (2 Corinthians 3:13–18). What are the implications of this for the way we use our iPods and other technology, given their capacity to shape who we are, how we think and who or what we are becoming?

Does being 'transformed into [Christ's] image with ever-increasing glory' (2 Corinthians 3:18) conflict with the new world created for us by the technological loop?

Does being 'transformed into [Christ's] image with ever-increasing glory' (2 Corinthians 3:18) conflict with the new world created for us by the technological loop? Are our new gadgets nothing but distracting toys, which provide interference in our search for God through Christ? Or is the technology 'neutral', meaning that we are as free to be Christians today as anyone throughout the ages – every age has produced its new challenges, whether through the advent of the printing press, or electricity, or the car, or the computer... Shouldn't Christians be able to use any technology in the pursuit of their relationship with God and for their own human flourishing?

We've already thought about pressing pause on our

iPods every now and then to create space in our life for reflection. Perhaps the same principle applies to our 'whole-life' engagement with technology. Sometimes, it's useful simply to switch off from the technologies that can distract or entertain or stimulate or divert you. So why not go for a walk, do some gardening, or write a letter and experiment with short but regular periods of techno-fasting (or jubilee, if you prefer). Why not, even in small ways, now and then, try to live like Jesus did – simply (Matthew 8:19,20)?

6 USE IT UP AND WEAR IT OUT

MUSIC, COMMODITY AND COMMUNION

The iPod world is a fun world, a beautiful world, a shiny world, a musical world. But isn't it also a world in which music itself, like everything else in life, has become a commodity; something to be traded, to be bought and sold, to be downloaded and shared, to be burned and ripped, to be stored and trashed at will?

Of course, music has always had a currency, with its own evolving industry and economy attached. But somewhere around the late 1980s and early 1990s, Western culture began to change in its attitude to this ever-flowing river of healing, inspiration and challenge. Our relationship with music shifted, perhaps imperceptibly at first. Music became more of a sound effect to be absorbed, rather than a culture to create and to participate within.

This is what Thom Yorke, of acclaimed band, Radiohead, told me when I interviewed him for *Third Way* magazine:

'Music has always been a commodity but now it's a commodity that's almost free – you can download it for a quid and you can do it through McDonald's, you can do it through *Metro* magazine or anything. I always felt that it was more valuable than that, and somehow at the moment it feels cheap. It's just so disposable. It's like, "I'll download another 50 tracks and listen to them once and then throw them away," that sort of thing. I find it sort of depressing.'

With music now readily available online, our attitude towards the way we buy music – and then begin to assemble it – has evolved. Once upon a time, of course, we bought albums – first on vinyl, then on tape, then

CD. Today, we can still buy albums as a whole if we want to. But more and more people are downloading just the tracks they really like, before assembling them into an ever-mutating playlist. This changes not only the way we listen to music, but also the way music is produced. There's now more pressure on artists to create individual songs of commercial worth, instead of making albums which you listen to in one go. If a song isn't instantly catchy, instantly memorable, it's likely to disappear without trace. You are freed from having to give attention to songs that don't grab you in the first few seconds – free (and it's easier than it's ever been) to pretend that David Bowie only made anthemic glam-rock singles, free to surgically remove The Style Council from Paul Weller's career, free to reduce the 'Messiah' to only the Halleluiah Chorus and free to cut anything Ringo ever sang on out of the Beatles' back catalogue. Has the iPod given personal whim absolute control over the world of music, totally erasing the role of patience, of careful listening, of tracks 'growing on you' or being hard work but worth it?

Has the iPod given personal whim absolute control over the world of music, totally erasing the role of patience, of careful listening, or tracks being 'growing on you' or being hard work but worth it?

We are growing used to inhabiting a disposable culture in which we place less value on art for art's sake. We tend to assemble the tracks we instantly take a liking to, and arrange them into different playlists on our iPods according to our own categories. The musician's art therefore becomes a tool that we use, a technological solution, if you like, to improve our mood, to lift us, or console us. We begin to lose the art of allowing artistry to challenge and shape us, to provide a window on the world which we need to look through. Instead, serious artists blur with karaoke culture and X-factor cover singers; they jostle with wedding singers and manufactured pop bands and dead musicians and re-issued albums. And the danger is that they dumb down their work or they get drowned out amid the white-noise cacophony of the entertainment world.

I remember that when I was young, our rather zealous church youth leaders would occasionally talk about the dangers of music, and about the way certain albums had been burned in America by Christians who wanted to renounce what they considered to be Satanic music and so make their lives pure. It certainly creates quite a spectacle, a little like the Nazis burning books in 1930s Germany. They even burned the Beatles. Today, such scenes would be all but impossible. In a world in which albums are electronic folders and songs electronic files, you don't destroy the music you don't want to consume anymore; you just delete it. So, does music really matter anymore?

The Archbishop of Canterbury, Rowan Williams, recently wrote the introduction to a Church of England report on the environment called 'Sharing God's Planet'. In it he wrote one very telling and helpful sentence in particular: 'We are not consumers of this world,' he wrote, 'we are in communion with it.' We all live within a consumer culture. Consumerism is like the air we breathe. It's like water to a fish. You can't see it; you can hardly detect it. It's a part of life and it's so familiar that we don't always know we're in the thick of it. But consumerism as a worldview affects the way we approach anything, from religion to music.

Jesus prayed that his disciples, though not being any longer 'of the world', might nevertheless remain 'in the world' (John 17:14–18). Doesn't it follow that whilst we find ourselves living in a culture of consumerism, we, as Christians, are not to be 'of' that culture? And doesn't that mean that it's crucial for us to resist seeing everything as a commodity – or, at least, as *only* a commodity? Of course, we buy and sell music – we have done for years. But how can we treat it with the reverence and respect that such a gift from God deserves?

Of course, we buy and sell music – we have done for years. But how can we treat it with the reverence and respect that such a gift from God deserves?

If we think of being in 'communion' with or through music, surely our approach to music must deepen? Should we therefore see ourselves as having a relationship to nurture, not just with the music but with the musician? And should we see music, ultimately, as something that connects us all, that provides a shared experience, and puts us in contact at a profound level not only with each other, but also with the Creator of all? Is the iPod revolution in danger of turning the divine, communal gift of music, given to be shared for the benefit of all, into a highly individualised commodity?

David wrote in Psalm 24, 'The earth is the Lord's, and everything in it, the world, and all who live in it'. Dwell, for a few moments, on that line. Ask yourself, what is my relationship to my things, to my many and varied possessions? The iPod, with its sleek curves and ergonomic lines, is a desirable consumer durable par excellence. But what does our ownership and use of an iPod (or any other technological gadget) tell us about who we are, how much we have, and how much more we want? And about the extent to which we really believe that the earth and everything in it is the Lord's? How might you go about being in communion with music rather than just being a consumer of music? And, more widely, how could you, as a child of God, become less a consumer of God's earth, and more deeply in communion with it? (*Connect: Climate Change* has much food for thought in this area.)

THE iPOD AND DISCIPLESHIP

The iPod shows just what a melting pot our culture is today. 'Youth culture' and the various subcultures which were once widespread, like 'Mods' and 'Rockers', has gradually given way to a myriad of micro-cultures, no longer solely for 'youth', from which we can pick and choose our various lifestyle options.

We assemble our lives like a playlist on an iPod, taking a bit of this and something of that and sewing it together to create something, we hope, that flows well and sounds good and makes some sense. It can be a deeply beautiful and creative exercise, allowing us to imagine our lives as a free-flowing creative act of self-expression. This, surely, should be an attitude we should try to catch hold of more often. Life doesn't always have to be a ladder to climb or a greasy pole to get up, does it? Can't it also be a river of music or a stream of endless creativity?

Life doesn't always have to be a ladder to climb or a greasy pole to get up, does it? Can't it also be a river of music or a stream of endless creativity?

But in our culture it's all too easy to adopt an exclusively consumerist approach to life, overuse our choice and our ability to delete those components, files and folders of our lives that we tire of or become bored with at any given time. Perhaps this is especially the case if our roots are not deep and we glide across the surface of culture without ever stopping to go deeper in any one place. Does such a way of living really suggest that we believe that anything we do has any kind of eternal consequences? Does anything we do – or create or commune with – last beyond us, and into the life to come?

Does anything we do – or create or commune with – last beyond us, and into the life to come?

As we've said, music isn't all about consumerism. And neither is life all about *superficial*, individualistic self-expression. Instead, it's about allowing our expression to flow from the *depths* of who we really are. If we are to live more deeply as lovers of God and lovers of music – and to express ourselves more powerfully – we need our hearts to be strong, to be one, to be generous, to be bold, and to be whole.

'Give me an undivided heart,' wrote David, 'that I may fear your name. I will praise you, Lord my God, with all my heart' (Psalm 86:11–12). And that's what everything boils down to in the end. For in the end, God wants to know what song will *you* sing? What lies at the core of your very being? What is in your heart?

God wants to know what song will you sing? What lies at the core of your very being? What is in your heart?

It's not ultimately about how cool our iPod or other MP3 player is, or how 'alternative' or cool our playlists are, how many gigabytes of storage we have, or whether we have the latest version of the newest technological toy in town. It's not about what we accumulate, or how fast we upgrade, or how much we consume. Isn't it, instead, about who we are, and how we commune?

'Search me, O God, and know my heart,' David, a uniquely musical warrior, also wrote, this time at the end of the beautiful song of praise that is Psalm 139. What is this, if not an expression of desire for the deepest possible communion with God? And, according to the Bible, this depth of communion composes songs that are in no need of an iPod to give them voice, songs from deep within us, songs that are the stuff of all that we can't leave behind. 'The Lord is my strength and my song,' sang Moses and the Israelites after they had miraculously crossed the Red Sea (Exodus 15:2). 'He [the Lord] put a new song in my mouth, a hymn of praise to our God' wrote David in Psalm 40 (a song adapted by U2 in their song, '40', incidentally).

Those who sing must also listen; those who listen must also sing. We are not consumers of this world, but in communion with it. Plugged into a different kind of 'matrix', a peculiar kingdom in which the first will be last and the last first; in which those who have never been heard before will be invited on stage to sing the song of their lives; in which we will dance in time with each other, and play in harmony. A kingdom in which the Creator will unlock our talents for evermore, to express who we are through ourselves and each other, to his glory, through technology, music, art, literature, dance, and every other good thing that he has given as a gift for the benefit of all Creation.

Sure, tell me what's on your iPod, but first ask yourself, what's on your heart?

Sure, tell me what's on your iPod. But first I'd love to know, what's on your heart?